Sociopath
both worl

counter attack their behavior

By Ken Fisher

Table of Contents

Chapter 1 – Differences in Sociopath, Psychopath, Sociopathy and ASPD

There is a vast amount of different disorders which come under the umbrella of mental health issues. These main types are:

• Anxiety – Anxious response to certain stimuli is a fairly common issue and is classified as a mental health issue.

• Mood – Extreme moods for long periods of time or very fast mood changes.

• Psychotic – This is usually displayed via seeing and believing in things which are not there; including hallucinations and delusions.

• Eating Disorders – Extreme emotional reaction to food.

• Addictions – People can become addicted to anything and this can have an extremely detrimental effect on their life.

- Obsessive Compulsive Disorders – Fear forces people to repeat a set of actions a specific number of times. The fear and the reaction are unique to each person.

- Post-traumatic Stress Disorder – This is the result of an extreme situation and can have long lasting effects.

- Personality Disorders – Society sets a standard of acceptable personality traits, based on the average person. People with a personality disorder exist on an extreme level of this range.

The sociopath is someone who has a personality disorder; they operate in the extreme range of the normal emotional response.

Sociopathy is simply the term for the disorder, whilst the term sociopath is used for a specific person with the sociopathy disorder. Many medical professionals have now taken to using the term Antisocial Personality Disorder instead of the word sociopath or sociopathy. This is simply because the disorder is far more complicated than the classic image which is often attached to the word sociopath or psychopath. Not all sociopaths are criminals; many of these people manage to live successful, productive lives. In fact, many people with this personality disorder are highly intelligent; it is this which enables them to understand other people and manipulate them according to their needs. Their intelligence and charisma in their public persona will allow them to become a leader in business, a high ranking political figure or even a celebrity. This is possible because of their intelligence and their inability to consider other people's feelings. There are several key distinctions between a sociopath and a psychopath:

• Organisation. There is a key difference between these two personality types. A sociopath will have no regard for other people's feelings, but they will be haphazard and reactive in their approach to any issue. In fact, many of their actions are spontaneous; one action leads to another and eventually gets blown out of proportion. A sociopath will live in the moment, regardless of the effect of that moment on the people around them. In contrast, a psychopath will be highly organized, every action they take will be carefully thought out beforehand. They will usually devise contingency plans and will remain cool and calm; whatever the situation.

• Attachments – Despite the inability to comprehend the effect of their actions on others, a sociopath is capable of forming a relationship with one other or even a small group. However, these relationships will revolve around the sociopath and can be exceptionally volatile. As well as being prone to angry outbursts, they are usually nervous and often agitated. The result is that many relationships are short term. In contrast, the psychopath will be completely unable to form an emotional attachment. However, they will be able to mimic these emotions in order to gain people's trust and achieve their own aims.

• Image – The sociopath's personality will usually result in them appearing disturbed; or at the least odd, in comparison to the average person. This will make others feel wary of spending too much time with them as they are unpredictable. They often move from job to job and even place to place. The psychopath is far more integrated into society. Their ability to act the part will enable them to build a family, hold down a good job and even build a business empire. However, all their actions will be based upon an act, as part of a grand plan.

• Cause – The cause of sociopathy is thought to be a result of nurture; the environment in which someone was raised. It is believed that this can have a serious effect on any person and influence the way they view life and other people. Anyone who has been subjected to a massive trauma, particularly in childhood, or even emotional and physical abuse is at risk of developing a sociopath personality. In effect, these situations encourage people to switch off their emotions and learn to distance themselves from both their emotions and other people. A psychopath is generally believed to be a product of nature. Research continues into this delicate field but it is thought that a psychopath has undeveloped areas of their brain, in particular, "The Prefrontal Cortex", the part which controls impulses and emotions. Whilst this disorder is usually something you are born with, it is also possible to damage your brain in an accident and develop a psychopathic personality.

• Danger Level – A sociopath will not understand the effect of their actions on others and will not feel any emotion if they harm others. However,since this is a condition that has been learned, and not acquired by birth, there is still an understanding of the rules and regulations in today's society. A sociopath will not believe these rules apply to them. However, a psychopath will have no regard for the law and are able to remove their actions from their emotions. They can reason that anything is permissible if it is necessary to achieve their goals. Even if the course of action they intend to take is particularly bad. This makes a psychopath very dangerous to those around them; in fact, many of the most famous serial killers have been confirmed as psychopaths.

- Education – A sociopath is usually lacking in concentration and is easily bored. This results in a lack of education when growing up. Children who rebel against the rules and regulations are often seen as antisocial, in the more extreme cases this is likely to be due to the personality disorder. In fact, as many as four percent of the population, have sociopath personalities. As adults they will often reflect the classic 'thug'. Someone with a psychopathic personality will have integrated with society and seen the importance of an education. They will generally be well educated and able to control their behaviour in order to bide their time and make their move at the right time.

The differences between the two disorders are relatively small; however, they are significant in understanding the condition and offering treatment. A sociopath, who is a product of their environment, needs to have a carefully structured plan to assist them in adjusting to a normal life. It is believed that the ability to display empathy is buried and not gone completely; this makes it reasonable to assume that with the right treatment, counseling, and even medication can help someone with this disorder to become more in touch with their feelings and other people's. A psychopath cannot be treated in the same way, as their brains are underdeveloped and the emotive response required is just not there.

Both disorders are recognized as being an antisocial personality disorder (ASPD). The media has also highlighted the connection between psychopaths and people who are criminals; it has even been seen in a host of movies, one of which, is 'Hannibal'. However, this book will enable you to recognize a sociopath and, by default, a psychopath; but this does not mean they are a criminal. There are thousands of people who live with antisocial personality disorder and never commit a crime. It is also worth noting that a psychotic personality is not the same as a psychopath. The psychopath can integrate fully into society and appear to have emotions; the psychotic person cannot; they are completely disconnected from society; these are the types of people who will hear voices; which may instruct them to commit crimes.

Both psychopathy and sociopathy are classified as antisocial personality disorders as people with these disorders are unable to react in what is perceived to be a normal response. Unfortunately, a sociopath is not aware that they are acting outside of the perceived norm; even if you tell them. This means they are unlikely to seek out treatment for a condition they did not know they had. A psychopath may be aware that they have the disorder but are unlikely to seek treatment unless they see it as beneficial for some reason. Even if they do seek treatment there is no guarantee that they will provide truthful information to the medical professional

What's the first thing that comes to your mind when you think of the word **sociopath**? Often thought of as the serial killers and criminals among us, sociopaths are actually more like average people than you would believe. That is until you get to know them and see what's hiding under the surface. Sociopaths are masters at blending in, and few realize their true nature until directly confronted.

Part of what makes sociopathy so fascinating to us all is how little we really know about it. The causes, motivations, and behaviors of sociopaths are so vaguely understood that you have likely met at least one in your lifetime and had no idea who you were crossing paths with.

The first and foremost characteristic of a sociopath is their total disregard for anyone else. We think of them as evil, but they don't really have malicious thoughts and feeling towards others, rather they simply don't care about anyone other than themselves. This allows them to objectify others, and act without regard towards anyone else's wellbeing. Sociopaths are missing that moral compass that keeps the rest of us on track, and that allows us to understand things from other people's perspective to feel empathy.

Sociopaths are generally extremely charismatic, they feel no guilt in manipulating others to achieve their own goals, and will happily lie to your face as long as they have a personal gain. They often have an inflated sense of self, and place their own needs and desires above everything and every*one* else. Sociopaths believe they are entitled to the things they want, simply because of who they are. They are also likely to inflate their own achievements and abilities, simply to feel superior, and to have you believing the same thing about them.

If and when they do feel emotions, a sociopath will only feel shallow imitations, if any. What may seem like expressions of love, happiness or even fear, are more likely copied from witnessing the emotional responses of others, rather than truly experiencing the feelings themselves. Sociopaths are master manipulators and can make you believe they are experiencing strong emotions of any type, when in fact inside they remain unmoved. This trait is often what makes many people think of the criminal element of sociopathy first. Just as they feel no strong positive emotions, likewise sociopaths have no experience with guilt, remorse or shame. Their ability to imitate without ever really feeling, can even fool lie detector tests.

However, there is one thing that sociopaths feel strongly. Underneath their cool indifference, sociopaths feel a deep seated rage, coupled with feeling deeply angry and resentful of others. This rage fuels their every action, and their belief that they have the right to act however they want and use whoever they want. Nothing and no-one are off limits for a sociopath. Because of their lack of emotional feeling coupled with anger, sociopaths have a constant need for stimulation, much of this behavior, the rest of society deems risky, such as extreme sports, gambling, or promiscuity. Verbal and sometimes even physical outbursts are normal, even common. Sociopaths have a constant need to 'live on the edge'.

Along with this often comes poor impulse control. Sociopaths will spend little, if any time weighing up the pros and cons of any action, or giving any consideration to consequences, both for themselves and others. "I just felt like it" is a common response when being asked, "why on earth did you take that particular action or behavior?" Drug use, both prescription and illegal, is common with some sociopaths, as is committing crimes, simply for the buzz. On the flip side, sociopaths cannot tolerate any perceived boredom or monotony. Anything that requires long periods of concentration or repetitive tasks and behaviors is nearly impossible for the sociopath.

More than just displays of sudden temper, sociopaths can act impulsively on decisions,whereby, regular people will spend weeks agonizing over. Ending relationships, quitting jobs, or even moving out of your home – these are all decisions that can be made on a whim, resulting from the central desire of the sociopath to achieve the constant and immediate satisfaction of their own desires. How their actions impact others does not even enter their minds. They live each day as it comes and rarely plan or worry about anything other than the most immediate future.

Along with this, sociopaths have poor control over their responses, especially to those they believe have or will harm them, or anyone that suggest that they are anything less than totally in control of everything and everyone. The slightest provocation is enough to set them off, to the point where anyone else involved in the situation may not even be aware that they've done something wrong. Sociopaths take offense very easily and can become extremely upset over things that normal people would not even consider as slight. When a rage overtakes them, it's not uncommon for a sociopath to inflict serious emotional and/or physical damage on other people. While they may seem out of control, a sociopath knows exactly what they're doing when they rage. To them, it is a natural response to what they view as a challenge or provocation and they feel no guilt or remorse over injuring or harming the person who dared set them off.

It's estimated that up to four percent of the population is sociopathic. That means one in every twenty-five people. Your class at school likely had more people in it than that of your workplace. The chances that you have already met a sociopath are high. So, why didn't you recognize them for what they are? The answer is relatively simple. We have been conditioned by many sources, the media, film, television, everyone – to view sociopaths as the evil serial killers, the rapists, and murderers lurking in the dark, and the con-man on the run. So much so, that we often don't recognize the real deal when we cross paths. This is to our detriment. So, what's really true about sociopaths and what is merely a myth?

Myth 1: Sociopaths are all violent

Unlike what we see on news reports and popular movies, the opposite is actually true. Most sociopaths are not violent, and in fact, most violent criminals are not sociopaths. The truth is that most sociopaths have a constant need for stimulation, and this can sometimes manifest in violent or anti-social behavior, but they are certainly not all serial killers and rapists.

Myth 2: Sociopaths are psychotic

Again, the opposite is true. A sociopath may act in opposition to society's norms, but they are not 'crazy'. They do not suffer from hallucinations or detachment from reality unless a second psychological condition is also present. While their actions may well disturb us, they are perfectly rational to the sociopath.

Myth 3: Sociopaths are all in prison

Again, absolutely false! In fact, the majority of sociopaths live in regular society. It's estimated that only twenty percent of the prison population is made up of sociopaths. However, it's worth noting that they are responsible for about half of the serious crimes committed. They are more likely to be in prison than an average person, but more sociopaths live in society than in jail.

Myth 4: Sociopaths are all men

While sociopathy is diagnosed more often in men, we don't really know how many women are out there with the condition. This may be because of how the condition manifests. There is not much research out there on female sociopaths, but this indicates that women may only exhibit one or two of the signs found in men, usually a lack of empathy and gaining pleasure in manipulation. Female sociopaths are less likely to engage in violent or impulsive behavior than male sociopaths, and thus may simply pass by unnoticed far more often.

Some researchers believe that sociopaths can form genuine attachments to a few select people. They will still lie, manipulate and hurt anyone else, but the selected few that they genuinely care about are safe from these behaviors. Others believe that, in opposition to a psychopath, a sociopath is more likely to act out spontaneously and inappropriately, with no thought towards the consequences. For many reasons, research into sociopathy is still new, and many varying opinions exist. Whatever the case may be, we can all agree that recognizing sociopaths in your life is essential to your personal health and safety, and perhaps even to your life.

Could you know someone who is a sociopath, be friends with one, or even be in a relationship with one and not know? It's actually extremely likely that you know at least one. Although they are not all dangerous criminals, all sociopaths have the ability to make your life extremely difficult.

Not all sociopaths exhibit all recognized behaviors of the condition, and each individual behavior can also be strongly or only weakly expressed. When taken together, however, these traits can help you understand the personality of a sociopath. Here are ten common traits of a sociopathic personality.

1. Sociopaths are charming. Despite popular culture references that portray sociopaths as madmen, sociopaths are actually charming individuals. Rather than being repulsive, they instead often draw people to them, appearing to be the type of guy (or woman) that you want to hang out with. They will also be well groomed, and often very fit and well dressed. Obviously, not all people who fit this profile will be sociopaths, but watch out for over the top antics and large appetites, for more than just food.

2. Sociopaths are spontaneous. Ever had a friend suggest after work that you all go skydiving that weekend, or maybe even just order the most obscenely expensive or outrageous thing on the menu, just to try it? Sociopaths are more spontaneous than most people, and they are also drawn to more intense, risky behaviors. They will often engage in an activity that most would find too risky or strange, and not even hesitate before doing it.

3. Sociopaths feel no guilt or remorse. It's not that they are repressing feelings, they simply lack the capacity in their brain to feel them at all. The lack of any ability to feel means that they have no sense of guilt or remorse. They can stab someone in the back or betray them without any second thoughts when it suits them, or do something, that furthers their own cause, then it's worth doing – even if someone else gets caught in the crossfire.

4. Sociopaths lie often and big ones. Sociopaths lie without guilt too and will say anything to 'win', at all costs. Sociopaths will lie massively, simply to win an argument, and will even make the rest of us seem silly .

5. Sociopaths only love themselves. When it comes down to it, quite frankly, the heart of it is that sociopaths are self-serving. They may feel a slight affection for some people over others, but only truly love themselves. You have to look carefully, though, sociopaths will feign any emotion, including love if it suits them to do so in that particular moment.

6. Sociopaths must win at all costs. Be it an argument, a corporate contract, or the affections of a girl, once a sociopath has decided they want something, they will do anything to make it theirs. If you get in their way, expect trouble.

7. Sociopaths are often highly intelligent. Sociopaths tend to have higher IQ's than the average population, and many are highly intelligent. This high IQ, coupled with their recklessness and lack of remorse, can make them extremely dangerous.

8. Sociopaths are master wordsmiths. Sociopaths are often extremely articulate, and have no problems defending themselves or their point of view, often with no prior warning or preparation. They will often talk in a kind of 'stream of consciousness' monolog style that can drag you in before you know it.

9. Sociopaths will never apologize. Or, if they do, they certainly do not mean it. In the mind of a sociopath, they are never wrong. It is simply impossible for someone else to be better at something, or understand something better than they do. If confronted with their behavior or actions, rather than apologizing, they will go on the attack.

10. Sociopaths are masters of control. Have you ever been a witness to someone receiving incredibly bad or upsetting news? A sociopath can experience something anyone would find highly emotional, and not bat a single eyelid. Similarly, they will also respond to what most would call joyous news with a blank stare. If you find yourself panicked or exuberant, and your friend or colleague seems to not even register the event, watch out.

As mentioned previously, not all sociopaths are criminals, or even appear to be anything but amazingly successful people. Sociopaths are often highly functioning individuals, which helps them to integrate successfully into society and are often very successful in any field they endeavor to join, both at work and in their personal lives. Sociopaths will go to extremes to excel, to a point where regular people would struggle to achieve the same heights. However, all this comes with a cost. Sociopaths often have few, if any, friends, and also struggle greatly to maintain any personal relationships. What you may interpret as genuine friendship is not sincere behavior on their behalf. They are keeping you around because you are useful in some way, either by providing companionship, or benefits and access to something or someone else. Once you are no longer useful, or the sociopath is tired of you, you will be abandoned.

At first, you may think there's no need to worry about meeting a sociopath. After all, at only 4% of the population, how damaging can they actually be? Surely, if there was any real danger, wouldn't we be warned by now?

As a point of reference, however, stop and think about these statistics for a moment. The eating disorder, such as anorexia nervosa, is something that we see endless press about it's damaging effects and prevalence in society. The actual rate of people affected is 3.45%, less than sociopathy. Schizophrenia, a mental illness that most of us are at least aware of, has it's equally and potentially devastating consequences,which occurs in about 1% of the population. So, for every person suffering from schizophrenia, there are four sociopaths; Do you still think it is not worth worrying about?

So, how can you recognize a sociopath when you meet one? Here are eleven red flags to watch out for in any relationship.

1. They try to manipulate you. Sociopaths use manipulation and deception on a regular basis. They can even lie just for the thrill, and to see what they can get away with. They also like to see the effects of their lies on you and revel in your reaction. Watch out for fanciful stories that seem too amazing to be true, or conflicting stories told at different times.

2. They are top dog. A sociopath is **always** #1 in their own universe. They are extreme narcissists and believe that the world, and everyone in it, owes them simply because of who they are. If they are constantly putting their own needs before yours, even when you've made it clear that you need their help in something, watch out!

3. No empathy. Have you ever told your best friend that your boyfriend just can't understand what you're feeling, that they seem to have no idea why you're so upset about something? Sociopaths cannot relate to the feelings of others, and can't imagine what it must be like to feel deeply about anything.

4. Never apologizes for anything, ever! A sociopath does not experience guilt or shame. Nothing is ever their fault, and an argument was simply their way of asserting their natural dominance over everyone. If you ever do get an apology, wait to see if your partner is just giving you lip service, in another attempt at manipulation.

5. Always calm and collected. Because they do not experience anxiety or guilt, situations where normal people may feel fear or stress do not affect a sociopath. Situations that you may worry about will be brushed off by a sociopathic partner.

6. Acts without thinking or regrets. Express an interest in going to Paris in your lifetime one day, and then discover that your partner is on a plane to Europe. Perhaps your partner has just blown your entire savings because he saw a good deal on that new flat screen TV. Sociopaths can be extremely impulsive, and act without any thoughts towards the consequences of their behavior.

7. You never meet their friends. Sociopaths do not have many friends, or indeed not any real ones. Unless a person is useful for them, there is no point in maintaining the relationship.

8. Charming only when it suits them. A sociopath is a master of disguise. Unless you know them well, you will often think they are the nicest guy out there. In fact, many women involved in relationships with sociopaths are greeted with disbelief when they try to tell their family and friends what their partner is really like. Remember, a sociopath always has a hidden agenda.

9. If it feels good, do it. Sociopaths can live by the pleasure principle. They require extreme and constant stimulation and seek pleasure from wherever they can get it. As well as risky and extreme sports, sociopath often takes great risks in other areas of their lives, including their sex lives. Sociopaths can be extremely promiscuous, and may not ever use protection.

For many sociopaths, it is definitely quality over quality. If someone you know has a large number of partners, and also perhaps engages in many one night stands or other 'sexually risky' behavior, it might be time to take a second look at being involved with them yourself.

10. Couldn't give a crap what people think. You may view this trait as appealing, but it's actually a sign of a darker problem. Sociopaths believe that society's laws and moral code do not apply to them. They do what they like, and couldn't care less what anyone thinks of them.

11. Everything is very intense. Another signal that many actually find romantic. A sociopath is extremely intense, not just about their relationship with you, but everything in their lives. They will often be full of passion, and hold eye contact for longer than you feel comfortable with. Everything about their life is as big and intense as their ego, and they are the center of it all.

If you are concerned about a friend, colleague or loved one, and notice more than one or two of the above signs in them, then it would be wise to be extremely careful in any future dealings with that person.

There are also other signs that can help you recognize the sociopath in your life. Sociopaths are masters of manipulation, especially when it comes to maintaining their own sense of superiority. You probably consider yourself a reasonably intelligent person, but you may find yourself doubting your own abilities frequently when in the company of your friend or loved one. They have no concern over your feelings, and so they will try to make you believe anything that furthers their own goals. A sociopath will turn around and flat out deny saying something or behaving in a way you are calling into question, to the point that you start to question your own beliefs and even sanity.

Be wary of someone who seems like a perfect partner for you, your soul mate – right off the bat. They smile across the room at you, laugh at all your jokes (even the dumb ones), constantly draw you in and wanted to hear your thoughts and opinions on everything. Then one day, suddenly they lash out – they don't want to know what you think. They might even get angry, or even physically violent, either to you or objects around you, if you challenge this sudden change in temperament. For a sociopath, rage is at their very core of being. It's not often talked about, but their sense of superiority coupled with their lack of remorse can lead to very angry confrontations.

How about other friends and associates? Have you been introduced to their family? Perhaps you can't understand why someone who is so lovely and charming could have so few other friends who recognize what a wonderful human being they are. Perhaps this is because the ones that came before you have already experienced their other side.

If you question this, sociopaths will lie. You'll be told how every girlfriend they've ever had did them terribly wrong, or how their entire family was taken out in a single, tragic accident, and that's why they're alone. There are ways to independently investigate such grandiose claims. If you're suspicious, do not take anything at face value.

Along with a similar line, watch out for anyone who tries to isolate you from your own friends and support group. Sociopaths like to remove you from any other support so that you don't have the ability to pull back or have someone else remove you from the situation and point out to you just how strange your new boyfriend is. Despite how glib and charming they can first appear, sociopaths are actually often socially immature when it comes to the crux of it. They can be extremely selfish and needy, to the point of obsession.

If you've confirmed that someone you know is a sociopath, then it's best to simply try and avoid that person as best as you can. If that person is in one of the regular circles you travel in, for example, a co-worker or friends with your other friends, then it may not be possible to avoid them completely. However, this doesn't mean that you should be openly hostile to the person when you do have to deal with them or tell them that you think they're a sociopath. This can actually put you in a dangerous situation, and make the person even more determined to 'win' you over. Simply divert the discussion where possible, or refuse to engage beyond simple replies to direct questions only.

Chapter 2 - Characteristics of a Sociopath

Your best friend or your neighbor could be a sociopath; this does not mean they are about to commit a crime, or that there is anything wrong with you. As already mentioned, a sociopath is able to connect with an individual or a small group. They will always be seen as the slightly eccentric member of the group, but, can have long-term relations if there is no reason for conflict to occur. Thus is an incredibly broad brush and may mean that one person in the group is regularly patching things up with the sociopath.

In order to recognize a sociopath it is essential to know and understand their main character traits:

- **Behavior**

A sociopath will behave according to what they feel is right and best suits their needs and desires. They will usually seek instant gratification and this will often lead to promiscuous behavior. As they have no interest in the effects of their actions they are happy to have sexual relations at any moment and anywhere. This is not an attempt to grab attention; it is simply the need to satisfy a carnal urge; regardless of where they are or who they are with. Whilst their behavior can be used to manipulate others; they are usually more subtle than this.

- **Feelings**

Sociopaths have very few if any feelings on display. This is a direct result of the situations they have been exposed to in their lives. Despite the building of relations with others, you will notice that they never truly feel happy or sad. Where you may celebrate a great victory or even shed a tear at a particularly moving event, they will not. It is possible that they will attempt to emulate your emotion in order to appear as part of the group, but this will simply be to help them 'fit in'.

It is also possible that they will develop feelings of attachment but these feelings and emotions will be shallow, superficial and help them to gain what they need. Unfortunately, a sociopath has no regard for the people and things which surrounds them, and this makes it extremely difficult for them to develop any real feelings. They can become experts at mimicking feelings and this can result in you believing you are helping them and continuing to do so. This is in fact, a clever way of manipulating you to ensure that you assist them with whatever they wish to achieve.

- **Abide by the Law**

As the average sociopath is not interested or even aware of normal social conventions and boundaries they are often found to be on the wrong side of the law. It is highly likely that a sociopath will indulge in law breaking behavior as they have no regard for the effect of their actions and simply indulge in any kind of behavior which suits their needs. Often, the activities which appear to be the most fun are the ones which are against the law and they will do these activities again and again without fear of the consequences.

- **Safety**

Unfortunately, a sociopath has no real concept of safety. In fact, to most sociopath's safety is not something that even registers as a concern. This does not just apply to their own safety; if their actions are likely to put others at risk, they are highly unlikely to register the danger and take any appropriate action. This is not usually a malicious action but simply a lack of awareness of the risks involved.

- **Aggression**

A sociopath lives in the moment; this can mean that they will react badly to a variety of situations. In truth, their actions are generally completely spontaneous and they can react extremely vicious if things do not go as they expected. This often translates into aggression. A sociopath is likely to become involved in physical violence and even assault others if they believe that a situation develops does not suit them and their needs. Their aggression will often manifest as threats and verbal abuse before they become violent; in fact, in the majority of cases, the threats are enough to make people react how they want them to. This behavior can be directed at anyone; regardless of whether you consider them a friend or not.

- **Spontaneity**

This is a key trait of any sociopath. They have an urgent need for instant gratification and this can make them extremely spontaneous. They may wish to try something different through boredom or because they see an opportunity to further their own interests. No matter what the reason they are likely to switch from one activity to another; disregarding any activity and the people that go with it, as soon as it loses its appeal. To an onlooker, it will appear that the sociopath is capable of starting a wide range of products but is not capable of finishing any project.

This effect is compounded by a sociopath's inability to plan for the future. The need for instant gratification and living in the moment means that they have no time to consider the long-term effect and will always fail to plan for the long term.

- **Empathy**

The lack of emotional response and an inability to appreciate the emotions of others and the effects of their actions is connected with the lack of empathy the typical sociopath displays. A sociopath is unable or unwilling to connect with others and to look at a situation through the eyes of another. This makes it extremely difficult, if not impossible to act in the interest of others. Of course, as a sociopath does not have the ability to connect with others they do not have any issue with acting in any way that suits them. This can be exceptionally convenient and make the decision-making process very easy as the only thing which needs to be considered is whether it will make them happy or not.

- **Deceitful**

When things go wrong a sociopath will happily pass the blame onto someone else; this can result in an issue if the other person does not wish to accept the blame! Creating a lie and building on that lie is something that a sociopath will do without thinking, the lie can be built upon until it is thrown out of all proportion. This will often lead to the exposure of the lie. The true sociopath will probably react with aggression when the lie is uncovered; they will quickly point the blame in a new direction and build a new lie to cover this redirection.

It is important to understand that these fabrications are products of a mind which is unable to comprehend the effects of lies on others. They are not usually deliberately designed to be hurtful; they are simply a means to an end. The usual aim for a sociopath is to establish a comfortable life; their deceit will be motivated by the need for monetary reward. In some cases, the deceit will be the result of the need to be accepted, although even this will be part of a larger plan.

Perhaps the most common method of deceiving people is to object if someone says they do not have good motivation; they will point at the actions they have taken and highlight that these actions are helpful to others and illustrate that they are good for people. This will probably make you feel guilty for questioning their intent and you will end up doing what they need to remove your own feelings of guilt.

• **Sense of Self**

Someone who is suffering from an alternative personality disorder, specifically a sociopath, has a heightened sense of their own self-worth and that this self-worth is the ultimate motivation for them to pursue any course of action. Their heightened sense of self-worth will lead them to see others as objects rather than people with needs and desires. This then leads to a lack of understanding of the need for personal space which most people possess.

The sense of self-highlights an interesting dilemma that is relevant to sociopaths, even if they are not aware of it themselves. A sociopath will not have a well defined moral identity; their actions are motivated by personal gain and not by the standard moral compass. This means that they will not be able to undertake any lifelong project because their time, patience and motivation will not support such a project. However, it is this type of project which can help anyone to have a more fulfilling, purposeful life. It is these projects which become part of a life and help to define a person and heighten their own self-worth. This is something that a sociopath wants to aspire, but they are unable to understand the basic need for personal identity and moral integrity which makes it possible.

- **Manipulative**

Sociopaths work at a much more simplistic level; they seek to manipulate those around them in order to achieve their own goals. Sociopaths do not have the moral boundaries that the majority of people do have. This means that they are able to use any method available to them to convince you to assist them; even if the method in question is violent.

Although most sociopaths are not good at planning for the future or even looking past the here and now; they will easily pick up on your fears and desires. Their ability to appear to fit in for short period will enable them to understand your motivation. This can then be used to inspire you and trick you into helping them; either by believing you are making yourself a better person or by believing it will genuinely help the sociopath.

Their manipulation tactics do not need to be malicious although they may be. As they do not understand the effects of their behavior they are guided by self-adulation and not the well being of others.

It is likely that a Sociopath will display all of the above traits and that these traits will have been visible since childhood. Of course, as young people develop, many of them will go through 'difficult phases'; this is a normal part of the development and can make it hard to spot anyone who has a sociopath personality type as opposed to being a teenager. As someone matures it becomes more obvious, although not easier treat.

Knowing the traits will go a long way towards assisting you to identify one if you should ever come in contact with such an individual. As already mentioned, it is highly likely that you have already met one and are possibly already being manipulated in ways you did not know were possible!

To assist in avoiding this or in dealing with the situation if it has already arisen, then it is essential to read the following guide for additional ways to spot a sociopath;

Charming

The average sociopath is surprisingly charming; they may come across as a valuable member of society who is only interested in helping and supporting others. Unfortunately, there are also plenty of people in life who are genuinely seeking to help others. This makes it exceptionally difficult to know if you are dealing with a genuine person or a sociopath.

One of the best places to start is to examine their 'facts' more closely. A sociopath will be a prevalent liar; if you are prepared to do a little digging you should be able to investigate some of the claims they have made. It will quickly become apparent that they have fabricated the information. Even if a specific outcome has happened it will not have been influenced by the sociopath, unless it suited their needs at the time.

Their ability to charm will probably also extend to an ability to make you feel at ease; they will be excellent at flattering you and you are probably likely to seek out their advice as they will imply they have a huge amount of worldly knowledge to impart.

Attraction

Many sociopaths will appear sexually attractive; this will be a result of their own feelings of self-worth which provides them with the appearance of self-confidence. It is also the product of a strong sexual appetite. This does not mean that all attractive people are sociopaths; but any with an excessive self-interest and an inability to consider other people's feelings could well be a sociopath!

Competitive

A sociopath will want to win, no matter what the activity. This is because they believe themselves to be better than others; making winning a foregone conclusion. In reality, this means that they will do anything to ensure they win, including, but not limited to, things which would be beyond the scope of most people's comprehension.

This is also apparent when someone attempts to destroy the web of lies they have surrounded themselves with. The first reaction will be to build more lies and defend their position; even if they start to contradict themselves. If this approach does not work they are likely to become aggressive and potentially violent. They will never admit to being wrong and a sociopath will never apologize unless they feel it is beneficial to them to do so. Even if this is the case it is likely to be a confusing story like apology, which will make you feel like you have been apologized to when you have in fact, not actually received an apology!

Wordsmiths

Sociopaths are generally very good with words; this enables them to talk about complex theories and to become excellent storytellers and, often, poets. This ability allows them to transfix the majority of people and dazzle them with their knowledge and command of the language. This is usually enough to convince the listener that they know what they are talking about.

In fact, they can often come across as hypnotic; their stories will seem real and will become so intriguing that you will be unable to resist listening to them and becoming absorbed by them.

Heroic

One of the most obvious traits of a sociopath is the ability to be the hero. You probably believe and hope you would do the right thing in a given situation and put other people first, becoming a hero in the process. However, in reality, there are very few opportunities where you are faced with these challenges and choices.

A sociopath will have appeared to have been in this situation many times and will have made the right decision to protect others, every time. This is a direct result of their ability to lie at any moment. If they are caught out looking after their own interests they will quickly spin the story to ensure it reflects them as a hero. In fact, many situations which require a hero, have actually been created by the sociopath and their inability to see that heir part in the process compounds this situation.

The first rule and the easiest approach when dealing with a suspected sociopath is to check the facts. However, do not ask those who are following the person to verify any information; they will be too under the sociopath's influence. Verify any claim independently, however, you should be cautious when approaching a sociopath with the truth; they will use their mastery of words to turn your own words against you. Sometimes it is better to establish the truth in your own mind and simply walk away.

Chapter 3 - Dealing with a Sociopath

There are many people throughout history who may be classed as sociopaths; although it is essential to remind yourself of the difference between a sociopath and a psychopath. Hitler is often mentioned as a sociopath, when in fact, he was more likely to have been a psychopath; his actions were calm, well planned and he held no regard for the lives of others.

Thankfully, people with such extreme mental disorder and the ability to obtain significant power do not come along very often. However, the sociopath is someone you could easily meet in an everyday scenario; you will by now, have realized that they are not necessarily easy to spot. Perhaps the most important factor to evaluate, is that, the best way to deal with a sociopath, if you should come in contact with one, is to simply avoid such an individual, providing that it is not mandatory to interact with them.

Information

A sociopath needs as much information as possible about you to ensure they can understand you and use you for their own gain. They will not be able to feel any empathy for you but they will be able to use any information concerning your life, ambitions, and personality to manipulate you and ensure you assist them with their own goals. You are unlikely to realize they are doing this; if you suspect someone is a sociopath and their traits match the ones listed here then it is best to stop providing them with any information about yourself.

If this is a colleague at work ,then you should be able to avoid discussing your own thoughts and feelings by simply returning the conversation back to them every time. They will be enthralled by the way you respond to them. Without additional information, they will be less able to manipulate you and you will be able to take everything they say and treat it with extreme caution.

Know Yourself

You may think that no one could possibly know you better than you know yourself; however, this may not be true. A sociopath can usually pick up on both your strengths and weaknesses. While it is a skill to exploit your weakness, it is often easy to spot, as you will frequently feel uncomfortable when completing a task on behalf of someone else. You will quickly realize that it is your weakest area and may even pick up on the fact that the same person is responsible for pushing you into a situation where your weakness is exposed. The result of this is, you react in a predictable way and that helps the sociopath to achieve their goals.

However, a more difficult skill to detect is when they are using your strengths against you. For example, you may be the sort of person who likes to help others. A sociopath will play to that strength, making themselves appear weak and in need of assistance simply to get your help. This has two benefits; the first is that they gain your trust as you are helping them out; they do not seem like a threat to you, and secondly, they will be able to ask you to do things for them in the future; under disguise. In fact, they will be manipulating you for their own ends.

The only way to avoid either of these scenarios is to know your own strengths and weaknesses completely. This will allow you to see when you are being manipulated and react accordingly.

End Contact; If Possible

It is not always possible to simply walk away. You are human and may feel a need or desire to help them; however; it is very difficult to help someone with sociopathy and not something that you should ever attempt alone. If the person you suspect or know is a sociopath is your boss, colleague or family member, it is unlikely you will have the option to simply walk away. In these instances it is best to consider all your options, starting with limiting your contact and being aware of how they may try to manipulate you.

If you are able to simply walk away then this is your best course of action. Your presence is likely to encourage the sociopath and you must rely on those who know them to do the right thing and attempt to help the sociopath. If you are concerned then there is no reason not to keep an eye of the person; just do it from a distance.

Knowledge is Power

Knowing they are a sociopath gives you the upper hand! You can choose what information to give them and you know that much of what they say is false. This should put you in a position to work out their aims and intentions and instead of falling into their well thought out plan or trap you should be able to outmaneuver them. However, be careful with this approach! You are not likely to be as manipulative or have as much of a disregard for other people as they will; if they realize you are trying to play them they may react violently or by resetting the trap to allow for your actions. It can be a dangerous game to play!

Professional Help

The only way to help a sociopath is through professional help. Unfortunately, it is usually very difficult to get a sociopath to see a medical professional as they will not perceive that there is anything wrong with them. It is not just the sociopath which can benefit from professional medical intervention; it can be a valuable source of support for you and will also provide an avenue to discuss the issues and make sure you are aware of any attempt made by the sociopath to manipulate you. This is much easier to stop and prevents if you have independent assistance.

It is highly likely that a professional will do more than just provide you with support; they should also encourage you to research the subject of a sociopath. Of course, most doctors will call the condition an antisocial personality disorder as they will not wish to provide a definitive diagnosis. This will leave you needing to understand the difference between psychopaths and sociopaths; thankfully this has already been covered in this book. It is important to learn as much as you can about the sociopath and how they operate; understanding their basic character traits; as already described, will allow you to protect yourself from their manipulation and give them assistance only when they either truly need it or when you feel it is necessary.

Beware of Accusations & Recriminations

A sociopath does not respond well to accusations and recriminations. They may make it their life work to simply make your life a misery. They are probably more likely to become very defensive, argumentative and then extremely rude and aggressive in order to overpower your words and even turn them against you. They will not give up until they have shown themselves to be more powerful than you. You may think or know that you have a valid point, however, once a sociopath starts to argue with you, they will change viewpoints and arguments frequently to ensure you end up confused about the point they are making, or that you are trying to make. You will end up losing the argument even though you may not be sure why.

If you are involved in an argument with a sociopath then it is important not to resort to any type of emotion, this is guaranteed to make the situation worse unless the sociopath has been hurt or wronged by your words and actions. In this type of situation, you should display the same level of emotion you would if you were dealing with a non-sociopath.

Ultimatums

The average sociopath works in power, the more powerful they feel the better. An ultimatum will trigger this response; they will either believe you are playing a game with them or that you are threatening them. The response will be similar to the one you will get if you accuse them of something or recriminate them. It is not something you want to start on a whim, you must be well prepared to undertake an argument with a sociopath, even then you are likely to lose!

Right and Wrong

In the same vein, a sociopath will never admit to being wrong; this is not something they generally adhere to as they do not adhere to the moral guidelines which govern what is deemed to be acceptable. Instead, a sociopath will see everything in terms of power. You pointing out a flaw in their power, will be a direct challenge to them and they will fight dirty, using every trick they know to ensure you are unable to question their judgment now or in the future.

Stand Firm

Despite the risk of inviting the wrath of your sociopath friend, it is important to stand your ground in debates. Sociopaths respond to power and you must stand firm when dealing with them. They need to know that you will not allow them to have power over you and that you will not allow yourself to be manipulated by them. At times, this may be more difficult than it sounds but it is possible to stand your ground without antagonizing them. If you find it difficult to stand firm or resist them when you are by yourself, then it may be useful to confide in a friend and have them present whenever you speak with a sociopath. This will make it much more difficult for the sociopath to generate a hold over you.

Bite Your Tongue

Not literally! A sociopath will often work by spreading rumors and stirring people against each other. This plays nicely into the fact that they like to be in control and manipulate other people. The most important thing to remember when dealing with a sociopath is that everything they say could be a lie or an exaggeration. Never take their word for granted and assume they have told you the truth. If they have shared some good or bad news with you then listen and check the facts before you react; you could save yourself a huge amount of embarrassment!

In the same vein it is also important not to let the sociopath control any conversation; if you do they are likely to take it where they want to go. This could lead you into a conversation about something that you are not comfortable talking to them about, or a subject that gives them more information on you. Avoid this by leading the conversation yourself. This should be relatively easy with a sociopath as you can keep asking them questions and getting them to tell you stories. Obviously, most of what they say will be hugely exaggerated but it will prevent any disagreements and avoid them manipulating you!

Plan Ahead

Whether you plan to change jobs, move out of a shared home, or even split up with a long-term sociopath partner, it is important to keep your plans to yourself. Allowing a sociopath to know your intentions will be an invite for them to meddle in your plans; this may be simply trying to alter them for their benefit or it may be more complicated. They may wish to humiliate and belittle you to ensure you do not carry through with your plans; especially if your plans will make life harder for them. Instead, make your plans, keep them to yourself and slowly implement them; once you have completed them, you can update the sociopath; it will be too late for them to affect the outcome.

Help

It is essential not to provide help or accept any offer of help from a sociopath. Doing so will leave you indebted to them and they will use this to manipulate you and ensure you do what they want you to do in the future. If you do become indebted to them, then you will have to make it clear what you are prepared to do to restore the balance and the timescale in which you are willing to do it. The best way to deal with any sociopath, if you have to interact with them regularly, is to show them that you will not be manipulated by them. Stay calm when dealing with them, tell them they are lying when they are and show them that they cannot influence you to do their bidding; you will make up your own mind concerning the right path for you and your life.

Dealing with a sociopath requires you to recognize the characteristics and then either avoid the person if possible or, if not possible, avoid playing the mind games with them. The only way to do this is to stand firm in your own beliefs and focus on your own needs and desires. A final trick to ensure you deal with a sociopath successfully is to remind them regularly that you spoke to an authority figure, such as a mental health professional about everything. Sociopaths are not generally comfortable with the notion of authority figures knowing too much about them and will be less inclined to deal with you.

Chapter 4 - Living with a Sociopath and being a Sociopath

Realizing that the person you love, or that a close family member is actually a sociopath is a daunting proposition. It will be made worse by the fact that the person involved will not know they are a sociopath and it is highly likely that the rest of your family are not aware of this fact. Sociopaths are also very good at appearing to be charming, friendly, lovable, and are often seen as the center of attention. This will make it exceptionally difficult for you to convince anyone else who already knows them well to believe you. If you attempt to push your reasoning on others it may well be you that is labeled as having a mental disorder, or at the least that you are jealous of your sibling or lover.

It can be very hard to discover that you know the truth about someone's condition but are unable to do anything about it. Especially when will start to become more aware of the way they manipulate those around them. Many of the options dealt with in the last chapter may not be open to you,you will be in regular contact with them and they already know all about you. It may be possible for you to break off all contact and start afresh on your own; however, this can be a difficult choice because it will probably involve leaving family members behind as well as the sociopath.

There are several options which can help you to live with a sociopath without them manipulating or taking over your life:

Professional Help

If you are unable to obtain professional help for the person suffering from sociopathy then it is still possible for you to seek professional help yourself. This will provide an outlet for your frustrations and your concerns; you may even gain some useful advice on how to deal with them on a daily basis.

Help does not need to be in the form of a medical professional, having a good support group of friends may be enough for you to vent your frustrations and talk tactics. The main purpose of this help is to ensure you do not become stressed or ill because of the worry and constant awareness of the sociopath's ulterior motives.

The level of help required will be dependent upon the level of involvement you have with the sociopath. If they are a family member it may be possible to limit the time you spend with them, if they are a partner then this could be more difficult and the support network will be essential.

Blame

Many people who live with a sociopath may have done so for years before they realize they have been manipulated and misguided. One of the first feelings that many of these people have when they discover they have been manipulated is guilt. It is natural to blame yourself for your behavior and the hurt you may have caused others. However, it is very important to understand that you were manipulated by an expert. They know how to play on your strengths and weaknesses and do so to ensure the right outcome for their needs and desires. In effect, they will have created an alternate reality for you which you believed and influenced your decisions. This belief was not a result of a weak mind, it was a result of the love you had and probably still have for a person.

Stage one in living with a sociopath, if you choose to stay with them; is accepting that you cannot change what has happened and that it was not your fault. You are, however, now aware of it and will ensure they are unable to manipulate you the future.

Reform

It is very difficult to reform someone who has no empathy for others and no feelings regarding the emotional and physical damage they do to other people along the way. This is something that is not possible without extensive professional help; it is not something you should attempt at home by yourself. The more likely outcome is that you will simply give them more ammunition to use against you. Treating these types of conditions must only be done in conjunction with medical professionals.

Devise a Plan

One of the best ways to stay sane and avoid the negative connotations of a sociopath is to devise a plan. Your plan should involve your aims and goals with accurate timelines and how you intend to achieve them. This plan should be looked at almost every day to remind you of where you are going and how you are getting there. The plan should never be shared with your sociopath.

The plan will give you something to focus on and this will help you to stay strong when dealing with the sociopath in your life. Repeating your aim in your head when talking with them will also ensure you are able to say no to them if their requests do not fit in with the plan you have drawn up. If you say no enough times, the sociopath will get fed up and find someone who is more willing to do their bidding and easier to use. If this leads them to end the relationship, then, at least, it will not be you that is to be blamed. If they choose to stay in the relationship you will have a better understanding of each other, although you will always have to remain on guard concerning his personality and attempts to manipulate you.

Focus

One of the favorite tricks that a sociopath employs is to use lots of hand gestures and even to touch you often. These are all part of the way they gain power over you. They are called, "distraction techniques" and are employed to confuse you and ensure you are not aware of what they are really talking about or that they are contradicting themselves. The point of these distractions is to gain your confidence and have you believe that they have told you something secret and confidential. In return, you will feel obliged to share something about yourself and this is where their power comes from. Everything they do is a game; a game that they must win at all costs and that you probably do not even know you are playing.

Professionals and others who have experienced living with a sociopath will tell you that the only solution is to leave them. This may be true, but it is often harder to do than it may appear. Firstly you will need somewhere else to go and you will need funds or a job to get started again. You will also need to consider children if there are any involved. Secondly, you will need to be prepared emotionally not only for the wrench of separation but for their attempts to get you back. Living with anyone, even a sociopath becomes comfortable and reassuring in its own way. Separating yourself from this is not an easy decision as you will be facing the unknown. Alongside this, the sociopath you are trying to escape from, will use emotional blackmail and other techniques to try and stop you from leaving; another way of showing their power over you. Being a human with emotions and empathy it is surprising how many times you will go back with them!

Being a Sociopath

To fully understand the reasons why you need to leave a sociopath it may be necessary to understand what it is like to live life as a sociopath:

The sociopath is devoid of morals, or you may prefer to say is lacking a conscience, however, they are not usually naive enough to not understand that they are different to the vast majority of people.

Initially, a sociopath will have problems with authority figures, they will be happy to commit a crime or other morally ambiguous activities without fear of reprisal. The reason they can do this is because they believe they are better than everyone else and can do whatever they like. At this point a sociopath can sound incredibly similar to a narcissist; someone who has a love of themselves above all else. However, a true sociopath is defined by a lack of remorse or guilt for their actions. It is this characteristic which makes them most dangerous as they are able to undertake any task, no matter how horrid. They will complete it if they believe it is essential to their progress. Progress to a sociopath is simply the display of power over others; the more people they control the more powerful they feel; many cult leaders have been diagnosed as sociopaths due to this affinity with power and the ability to control others.

Being aware that they are different actually allows them to exploit others and what they perceive as weaknesses, a sociopath will not react in certain situations as a non-sociopath would. They usually have no fear and will simply see the challenge, not the consequences.

Living as a sociopath means that everyone in your life is an object; your aim would be to have power over them, to control them and use them to do your bidding. Often this revolves around making life easier for the sociopath. You would not be able to form any meaningful long term relationship as you do not have the emotional capability of non-sociopaths, however, you would still not want anyone to leave your circle as this is an affront to your power. It is for this reason that you would manipulate others and emotionally blackmail them to ensure you retain that power. In effect, you win the game. When people are no longer of any use they are simply dropped and left to put the pieces of their lives back together.

Living as a sociopath gives you an unusual power over others, you are able to see the world without emotions, this allows you plenty of opportunities to plan and scheme over the best way to achieve your aims; where emotions and fear of hurting other people will stop most people from doing something you will not falter. It is this skill that can make you a great leader, although not necessarily a nice one.

Every opportunity to meet people will be embraced, not because of the need to make a connection with others but because it provides another opportunity to exert your power over others. It also gives you the chance to explore and learn more about personalities; this will help you to understand the human psyche a little better than you already do.

Of course, the lack of guilt and the ability to charm and flatter people, does not mean that you will become a manipulative danger to society. There are many sociopaths who exist making all the right sounds and signs whilst holding down a good job and simply watching people. If you are one of these you may always feel like you are looking through a one-way mirror; watching people and analyzing them without them being able to see what you are doing. You may use your ability to manipulate people to help you obtain what you need, but not be dependent on controlling them long term. Instead of using a person to assist you and provide you with a feeling of power, you are more likely to see everyone as a part of your game. Each person has a role to play in supporting you.

In many ways a sociopath can actually be likened to a major celebrity or world leader; as long as they are popular, then people will put up with a huge range of issues; believing they are for the greater good. Perhaps the real question should be, can a sociopath live a normal life and still feel happy and fulfilled?

Chapter 5 - Treating a Sociopath and the Long Term Prospects

There are many people who say it is not possible to treat a sociopath, that, in fact, treatment simply gives them the opportunity to study human nature and devise new ways of manipulating people. There are several issues with this line of thought:

- **Opportunities to study are everywhere**

Whilst it may be a valid argument that counseling sessions will provide a sociopath with an opportunity to study human nature, this is not the reason counseling usually fails. The sociopath can study human nature anywhere, in libraries, on the internet and with people strolling down the street. In fact, studying people and working out their strengths and weaknesses is one of the favorite pastimes of a sociopath. They do not need to visit a counselor to gain this knowledge.

If a sociopath instructed to visit a counselor and has no other option then this will be part of the game to them.

- **Condition is through Nurture**

The majority of research points to sociopaths being a product if their environment. Whilst there may be an inherent brain issue at birth, the deciding factor is the lifestyle and treatment they receive as children. In fact, there are many cases of sociopaths who are only mildly sociopathic simply because they had a good parent balancing out the effects of the bad parent. Of course, as with much of the research, it is difficult to prove certain details.

The crux of the matter is that if a condition is a result of the events they have been exposed to, then it should be possible to work through these memories and gradually reconcile them; allowing the sociopath the opportunity to reverse the effects of nature. This may seem a little far-fetched but this is achieved every day when counseling helps someone suffering from post-traumatic stress return to a normal lifestyle. War veterans are some of the most likely candidates which spring to mind. If they can be taught to move past the events they have witnessed and the deeds they have done; there is still hope for a sociopath.

• The right of every human to receive medical assistance

Every human has a right to medical assistance when they need it. Whilst it is very rare that a sociopath will voluntarily seek help for a condition that they do not realize they have, it remains a possibility and one that should be taken seriously.

In fact, there are several methods which have been used to treat sociopaths, some of which have been tried and have proven to be unsuccessful:

• Counselling

Most attempts at counselling have proven to be unsuccessful; this is usually attributed to the desire to learn more about human nature than dealing with treatment. However, the real reason that treatment usually fails is a lack of respect for the counsellor. A sociopath will, by their very nature, attempt to outmanoeuvre and overpower their counsellor(mentally) . Once they have done so, they will lose all respect for the counsellor and the treatment sessions will become an amusing game,evidently, there will be no benefit to the sessions.

- **Tough Love**

The idea of telling a sociopath exactly what they are, what they do and how they affect other people will never help to cure them! Tough love relies on the principle that the recipient will feel guilt and realize the error of their ways. Unfortunately, this is not an option for the sociopath. They do not feel guilt, and any attempt to make them see the damage they cause to others emotionally, will simply be beyond their comprehension. People are objects and emotions and guilt are alien to them; they can simply not understand the point you are trying to get across.

- **Punishment**

This approach has been tried on numerous occasions and is often used when people are unaware they are dealing with a sociopath. By their very nature they have no fear of consequences and prison is simply another opportunity to exploit and manipulate people. Without being able to feel remorse or guilt they will find it impossible to learn from their mistakes. Even if they have already paid a visit to prison, a repeated experience will not concern them. It will, of course, give them the chance to learn new tricks and skills to complement their ability to manipulate people.

- **Medication**

Although there have been several trials with different medications there has not yet been a successful one. At present, there is no medication which will cure this disorder and the likelihood of this happening is far-fetched. This is because not enough is known about this disorder, how it occurs and how it affects the brain to be able to create an appropriate cure or long-term treatment.

- **Teaching Emotions**

In theory, if you could teach someone to feel something then you would be able to teach the sociopath to feel the pain they are causing and to even feel guilt. However, emotions are not something which can be taught; even the best artificial intelligence created has programmed responses, not real emotions. The same is true for the sociopath; you can educate them as to what emotions are and why they are important, but they will not be able to feel them. Teaching them emotions will simply improve their ability to manipulate others.

The following methods have been shown to have positive results and are, at present, the best way of treating a sociopath:

- **See and confronting the problem as a whole**

It is often the case that a sociopath will be treated for symptoms of the disorder or even other issues; they are rarely seen as one problem and this is essential to ensure you can make some headway against the disorder. Attempting to change one element of a sociopath is pointless; they will simply revert to form as it is part of their make-up. To achieve any positive results you must deal with the condition as a whole and confront it head on. Do not pander to the patient in any way; simply tell them the issue and how it can be resolved. Thus is a very long, frustrating road!

- **Systematic Integration**

The most successful treatment attempts are the systematic ones. Treatment is introduced into every area of their lives. This may require multiple counselors, co-operation from friends and family or possibly the dedication of one person. The idea is to integrate the treatment into their life and effectively show them the correct way to behave and how to treat others. This method has been shown to be successful although patients will often revert to form after initial improvements have been made and the treatment is scaled back. As it is not possible to have someone chaperon a sociopath for every moment of their lives this method is of limited long term use.

- **Education**

Sociopaths are often intelligent but may have become bored too quickly to pay attention in school and can actually be lacking in education. This is in contrast to the normal profile of a psychopath who will make the effort to appear normal in order to achieve their aims and are usually highly educated.

Although educating a sociopath may simply provide them with a better understanding of human nature and how to manipulate people, it can also have the opposite effect. Understanding the effect of their actions on other people does not require an emotional response. Educating the sociopath to understand there are other ways of achieving their aims, without manipulating people may encourage them to use different methods. This is particularly true if they are also educated as to how people can help them again further in life if they have not been alienated in the past.

- **Counselling**

It has already been established that counseling is of little if any effect when dealing with a sociopath. However, it is a valuable tool in dealing with sociopaths. The family, friends and anyone who is in regular contact with the sociopath will benefit from counseling.

In the first instance, counseling can be useful to help them get over their own behavior whilst under the manipulation of the sociopath. But more importantly, counseling can reinforce the future behavior around the sociopath and provide support to those who cannot simply leave a loved one; no matter what they have done.

The Future prospects for treatment and sociopaths.

Most experts agree that the best way to avoid being targeted by a sociopath is to appear emotionally strong and to avoid all contact with them. However, this is not always an option and may not be entirely fair to the sociopath.

Research is continuing and there is hope that one day, a cure or effective treatment method will be found. However, in the meantime, there is little that can be done to help the sociopath unless they wish to be helped.

Although research is continuing there is still very little known about the disorder and this makes it extremely difficult to provide any treatment. Currently, this means that sociopaths will continue to act in the same way they do, as they know no different. The majority of the information available on the internet and in books, centers on how to diagnose a sociopath and how to escape their clutches, if you have been under their spell. There is very little information on what it is like to be a sociopath and how to live with this disorder in the future. The reason for this is that most sociopaths are not aware that they are one; unless it is pointed out indirectly to them. Even if this happens they are likely to read it with some interest; identify the symptoms and then file the information away for future use. Knowing they have the disorder simply reinforces the fact that they are different and they know it; adding to the feeling of superiority they already possessed.

Perhaps the most encouraging story is that of neuroscientist James Fallon who accidentally discovered the neural activity in his brain was a match for the neural activity in the brains of several murderers and serial killers. It was also completely different to the neural activity in the brains of his family members. James was not aware that he was a psychopath although he did often do dangerous and reckless activities. He also held down a good job and had forged a career as a neuroscientist. This suggests that it is possible to live as a sociopath or psychopath without manipulating and hurting those around you. The question is how did James Fallon manage to achieve it and what can be learned from his experiences to aid others who are suffering from this variant of antisocial personality disorder?

Chapter 6- **Surviving a Sociopath**

But what if the sociopath you suddenly recognize is your boyfriend or your husband? What do you do then? The first thing to do is to open your eyes and stop being taken in by their charms. Sociopaths will commonly try tricks or stories to make you feel sorry for them, or manipulate you into falling for them. Recognize the tactics for what they are, and not genuine actions in a loving relationship. If you are in a relationship with a sociopath, and you've decided that it is not redeemable, then you need to get out as quickly as possible. You need to do this safely, but the longer you wait, the more you can be sucked into the sociopath's way of thinking, and the harder it can become to leave.

Remember that just because someone has treated you badly, or has done something you don't approve of, this does not necessarily mean they are a sociopath. A true sociopath will display more than one of the traits explained earlier in this chapter, and usually, will have aspects of nearly all of them in their personality. A true sociopath does not care what anyone else thinks or feels and does what they like regardless of who they hurt in the process. This is different from just dating a jerk.

Contrary to what you may think, sociopaths will usually target women who are caring and kind. Sociopaths are looking for a relationship where they can take without giving anything in return, and it is much easier for them to do this in a relationship where the other person is genuinely kind and giving, rather than another who is only out for themselves.

In the beginning, being in a relationship with a sociopath is like every girl's dream. Your partner is very easy going and relaxed and is a delight to be around. They say all the right things and are interested in everything that you are. You start to think you may have even met your soul mate. Like everything in the life of a sociopath, the relationship will be very intense right from the beginning. Nothing will be too much trouble, from running errands, to organizing reservations at your favorite restaurant. They will shower you with flattery, attention, and even gifts. A sociopath will sweep you off your feet before you've even realized what's going on.

Then suddenly, one day everything changes. A romantic relationship is just another opportunity for the sociopath to be in charge, to find someone who will buy into the game. Once they have you, the challenge to conquer has been met, and they are already moving onto their next target, while keeping you strung along. Sociopaths are often involved with more than one partner at once. Where once you were the center of their universe, now someone else has caught their attention, and you will only receive enough scraps of attention to keep you hanging on, until they're ready to move on to the next victim.

At this point, you may find yourself accepting worse and worse behavior from your partner, as they try to see how much they can get away with. Particularly if you do not know you're involved with a sociopath, you will have little idea what's really going on. Therefore, you can often find yourself accepting excuses or ridiculous stories that you would have scoffed at in the beginning of the relationship. Fearful of losing your 'soul mate' you may also change yourself to try and recapture that perfect relationship you had at the beginning. What you do not realize is that what you see now is the true personality of your partner, and the beginning of the relationship that you're clinging to was pure deception.

If you are truly dating a sociopath, and have decided that leaving is your best option, then you may want to consider ending the relationship from a distance, such as by phone or a letter. Face to face, it may be difficult for you to leave, as the sociopath can refuse to take no for an answer, and may even try desperate or violent methods to get you to stay.

If you do manage to escape the relationship, under no circumstances you should ever go back, after the initial breakup, you should expect the sociopath to try and win you back. A sociopath will turn on the charm again, trying to woo you as they did in the beginning of the relationship. If that doesn't work, you can expect a pity party or more amazing stories. Remember, this person knows exactly how to hook you in. They have spent months, or maybe even years, learning all about you and cataloging every one of your weaknesses. For them, trying to win you back is all about a game they can play. However, you must be careful, because if they decide they cannot win, a sociopath may try to punish you or become angered and violent around you if you do not give in, or if you start dating someone else. They do not even necessarily want to destroy what matters to you because they want it for themselves, but just to 'put you in your place' and have the satisfaction of being the one that took that thing from you. Take more care and pay attention when ending a relationship with a sociopath.

Finally, understand that you were not ever able to, and will not be able to control the way that the sociopath acts at the end of the relationship. Sociopaths usually have a string of failed relationships behind them. The inability to form real loving relationships is something that they simply cannot do. They will however never share this with you. Remember the stories they told you all about the crazy ex that just wouldn't leave him alone? Even if you disengage from the relationship successfully, the story he tells his next partner will likely be yours.

After you've left a sociopathic relationship, it's important to recognize the impact that it can have on you, therefore, take some time to heal. The effect of being taken in so dramatically has even left some wondering how they will ever trust anyone again. It's important to recognize that your trust, and innermost sense of self, was violated, and how to make sure you never find yourself in that situation again.

Firstly, it's important that you speak to someone. A therapist can be excellent at helping you sort through anger and grief at the betrayal, and I asure you,those feelings will come. You may also have been convinced by your partner that in the end, everything about why the relationship failed was your fault. A therapist can help you work through this and see the truth, giving you skills to understand and work through these feelings.

Once the relationship is over, disengage completely. Do not call them, or even send an email or mention something to **or** about them on social media. Remind yourself how hard you worked to be able to leave the relationship safely, and that no good can come from being further involved with this person. Many find that the longer they are separated from the sociopath, the more they see through the lies of the relationship that was always there behind the veil.

It's also important to make sure you're safe. Even if you never gave them a key, get your locks changed. You should also strongly consider changing your phone number. If you can, it's a good idea to install a security system or camera in your home. Finally, if you have any reason to fear for your safety, it may be best to stay with a friend or even consider moving.

While undergoing all this upheaval, document everything. This can be as simple as keeping a journal or saving any emails or text messages you get from the sociopath. Everyone hopes that it will never be needed, but if the situation does come to the worst, having everything available and documented will help with any court orders or getting the police involved if necessary. It's not uncommon for both property damage and assault to occur after you break it off with a sociopath.

Lastly, do not blame yourself. Sociopaths are highly skilled at reading people, and then manipulating them into doing exactly as they desire. What you can see now may be vastly different, but it does not mean you did anything wrong at the beginning of the relationship. They were trying to charm and woo you on purpose, and they are extremely good at it. Surround yourself with those who love you, and take comfort in the company of true friends and family. If you feel you want to, there are also support groups you can join. Remind yourself daily that most people in the world are good and honest, and that you can move on with your life. There is no future in this relationship.

What sociopathy is exactly, or even if it exists at all, is a hotly debated topic among researchers and mental health professionals. What most can agree on is that at its most basic level, sociopathy is a condition where people are emotionally disconnected from others. They do not have either the desire or indeed even the capacity to connect with other people. This then exposes them to a level of remorseless and antisocial behavior, the condition removing inhibitions or social responses that usually curb such behaviors.

Because sociopathy is usually recognized, and indeed often only diagnosed in a criminal setting, we know relatively little about sociopaths who have not engaged in criminal behavior. They do not often come to the attention of authorities, and many spend their entire lives without even recognizing for themselves that they are sociopaths.

Recent thinking on sociopathy is exploring the idea that the condition should be diagnosed on a spectrum. Rather than saying that you are a sociopath or you're not, it should be recognized that the condition is made up of many individual traits, of which not all need to be present for the individual to display sociopathic behaviors. From there, each of those traits also has a spectrum within each one. None of us is 'all good' or 'all evil', and even sociopaths can vary with severity within the condition.

One diagnostic tool used is a checklist developed by a Canadian psychologist named Robert D.

Hare. A revised version of the checklist is still in use today and is the tool that most health professionals use to rate or evaluate sociopathy and psychopathy. It consists of twenty personality traits and behaviors and should be used over time with a full interview and a review of other records and information available. Experts caution against the checklist being used by laypersons to try to identify or diagnose suspected sociopaths in their own lives.

A distinction some researchers made between psychopathy and sociopathy is the suspected cause. Some believe that a psychopath is born with the condition, while a sociopath is made.

What then causes someone to become a sociopath? We've all heard the stories about children who torture small animals, or continually physically hurt younger siblings, but not all children who display antisocial behavior will group up to become a sociopath, and conversely many sociopaths had perfectly happy and normal childhoods.

Many researchers and psychologists now believe that sociopathy is caused by a combination of both genes and environment. It's not just the genes that matter, but the individual's expression of those genes. You may have in fact inherited a gene, but your individual makeup and experiences mean that you never express that gene. In this case, is there any difference between you and someone who does not have the gene at all?

The study of epigenetics looks at the changes in your genes by external influences and experiences. We now understand that just because your body inherits a particular gene, it does not mean that this gene will influence you in any significant way. A change in the gene can be influenced by many factors, including age, the environment and lifestyle you experience, and other diseases.

So, perhaps children are born only with the *potential* to become a sociopath, and it is their life experiences that shape them this way. A small study of just eight boys in a residential program may give us a glimpse into possible causes. Traits that were common in psychopathic children were:

- Having a mother who was also abused or neglected herself

- An absent father

- Having little or no emotional connection to their mother

- Low birth weight or complications at birth

- Unusual reactions to insults or feeling of pain

- Lack of any attachment to any adult

•Failure to make eye contact when touched

•Low tolerance to frustration

•Exaggerated sense of self-importance

•Forms only transient relationships

•Displays cruelty towards others, both people, and animals

•Has no remorse when hurting someone else

•Expresses no empathy in friendships

A professor from the University of New Orleans named Paul Frick has created a list of ten warning signs he has identified as being present in children who may have psychopathic tendencies. These traits are:

•Persistently hurts, bullies or fights others. May also steal or vandalize other's property.

•Breaks major rules, such as staying out past curfew

•Shows no guilt when they are in trouble for doing wrong

•Has a persistent disregard for anyone else's feelings (not just siblings)

•Persistently does not care how they perform in school, even when expectations are made clear

•Comes across as cold and unfeeling, and only uses emotion to manipulate

•Does not accept responsibility for mistakes, and instead, blames others

•Has no sense of fear, and participates in dangerous activities

•Are not bothered by threats of punishment

•Highly motivated by what they'll receive, even if the action will hurt others (eg: stealing something)

Other studies have also supported the view that sociopaths are made and not born. A study performed by Dr. David Lykken has suggested that traits in children indicative of future sociopathy can, in the right environment, be redirected towards behaviors that society finds more appropriate. Perhaps this is where future Wall Street stock traders and extreme athletes are made. Today, more and more psychologists support the idea that, if caught early enough, sociopathic traits and tendencies can be limited, or even reversed, in children.

Some researchers believe that they have discovered a gene that may be the cause, or at least high contribute to sociopathy. This gene, combined with socio-economic factors, may be a significant cause of sociopathy. It is estimated that 59% of African American men, 56% of Maori men and 54% of Chinese men carry the gene. The rate in Caucasians comparatively is 34%.

Nicknamed the 'Warrior gene', the gene controls the production of enzymes that are part of the breakdown of neurotransmitters such as dopamine and serotonin. Therefore, this gene can influence feeling, moods, and behavior. The Warrior mutation means that people are less able to control levels of the neurotransmitters in their body, and can, therefore, express extreme and violent behavior. However, most believe that more research is required to make any concrete determinations. Interestingly, it's estimated that one in three men carry at least a shortened version (and therefore less active) version of the gene. Some researchers now believe that this may be the cause of anti-social behavior in many men.

Rather than being influenced by genetics, a secondary cause of sociopathy can be physical damage to the brain, either present from birth, or as a result of an accident. Previous research has linked head injuries or defects in the brain with a predisposition to violence. Concurrently, people who are either born with or experience early damage to their prefrontal cortex may never fully develop moral and social reasoning and understanding. Another part of the brain called the amygdala, when damaged, may impair the ability for the prefrontal cortex to understand feedback from the limbic system, which may result in an increase in violent and aggressive behavior.

Whatever the cause, the vast majority of scientists and professionals believe that the driving force behind sociopathy is the inability to relate to any other person. Without the ability to form meaningful connections to other people and to have any empathy or understanding of their needs and desires, all other behaviors linked to sociopathy suddenly become possible.

Chapter 7- **Is there a Cure?**

So, can sociopathy be cured? Most believe no, but there are some who believe it can be at least treated. However, there are obstacles in the way of treatment and improvement for sociopaths.

Firstly, there is the lack of a true understanding of the condition. We've all heard the term, but how many people really understand what a sociopath is? The answer is likely very few. There is not even currently a clinical diagnosis available for the condition, and so instead, it is a name for someone with certain traits, the key of which is the inability to feel guilt. Some have even gone so far as to state that with up to one in every twenty-five people exhibiting the condition, perhaps sociopathy is not a disorder but simply a normal human personality variant. In fact, in some areas society welcomes the sociopath. Who better to ask to defuse a bomb, remove that 'inoperable tumor' from your head, or even be a spy or sniper. They may not be your first choice of person to have over for a beer, but the person with the need for high stimulation, cool under pressure, and highly motivated by reward can be very useful in certain situations.

The second problem with seeking treatment is the amazing ability of the sociopath to fool the therapist. A sociopath is a born liar. They can manipulate and con their way through any situation. Should a sociopath find themselves in therapy, they would have little trouble deceiving all but the most experienced psychologist. Often, in fact, a whole other approach is recommended for simply dealing with sociopaths than with the general public. This can also lead to the sociopath quickly losing any respect for the intelligence of the therapist, which can make further treatment impossible.

The third problem is the inability for 'regular' non-sociopathic people to truly understand and empathize with the sociopath. Just as they cannot feel anything for others, we cannot turn that part of us off. For most people, the ability to feel emotions and empathize with others is such a deeply embedded part of our very nature, it's impossible for us to imagine what life would be like without it. We simply cannot imagine hurting, or even killing, another human being, and then simply feeling nothing. We can theorize and understand the behavior on an intellectual level, but the only person who will truly understand what it is like to be a sociopath are sociopaths themselves.

Finally, the last obstacle to treatment is that sociopaths themselves are highly resistant to change. After all, they view themselves as perfect. They see nothing wrong with their behavior, and to this point, it has probably served them quite well. Because sociopaths cannot understand feelings or what having them may be like, it is very difficult for them to imagine what life would be like being the other way. Society has also set up a stereotype where putting yourself first and going after what you want, no matter what the consequence is seen as a good thing to do. Ruthless people do very well in life, being it in the boardroom or the battlefield. There are even reality shows where people are lauded for the ability to come out on top after screwing everyone else over.

While it is debatable whether there will ever be a cure for sociopathy, some research has shown that it can be managed. Sociopaths respond poorly to threats of punishment or loss, but research has shown that they can respond well to incentives. A theory is that sociopaths will not be murderers and criminals simply because of who they are. Being a sociopath can make you cut off, callous or even violent, but it doesn't make you kill. In fact, it has been shown in some cases where the sociopath can see a benefit in 'playing along' with society, they can be a productive and fulfilling member of it. Rather than trying to teach the sociopath how to feel emotions, an impossible task where all they end up doing is learning how to mimic it, instead the theory is to accept a sociopath for what they are and approach them with logical processes and theories that explain why it is in their own best interests to act as society expects.

An interesting case to illustrate this theory is that of James Fallon. Although he calls himself a psychopath rather than a sociopath, his story is an extremely interesting one that gives a lot of insight into how sociopathy can be managed, and those with the condition can lead a fulfilling life.

Fallon is an American neuroscientist, and when he was researching Alzheimer's disease, he used brain scans of healthy family members as controls in his research. At the same time, he was working on a side project examining the brain scans of murderers who had been diagnosed to be on the psychopathic spectrum. Going through the scans one day, something caught his eye. By examining the films from the brain scan, he immediately thought that one of the scans from the killers had accidently been placed in the Alzheimer's pile.

Each scan was identified with just a number, and so Fallon had to ask a technician to look up who the scan belonged to, so it could be put back in the correct place. When the answer came back, Fallon is so shocked that he insists that it is checked again. However, no mistake had been made. The brain scan that so closely matches those belonging to psychopathic murderers is his. It is Fallon's scan of his own brain.

Fallon took a time to absorb the shock of this discovery because until that moment he had never thought of himself as having any sociopathic or psychopathic traits or tendencies. He then decided to ask around and found that rather than reassuring him, his close friends and family were not even surprised by the scan's results.

His parents shared stories of him from his childhood, where he was a little 'off', and he began to recall, that when he was younger some of his friends were even forbidden to play with him. Those he had a current relationship with nearly all had a memory to share where he had done things they considered to be extremely irresponsible or hurtful. For example once on a holiday, he took his brother on a hike to a cave in Kenya that Fallon knew was considered to be the origin of Marburg virus, a deadly disease. He knew, but his brother didn't, and Fallon believes that his brother will never truly trust him again. He's also taken his son fishing in an area in

Kenya where 'Beware of the Lions' signs were posted. When confronted with these behaviors, he was amazed that people were hurt by it, or considered that he had been harmful to those he loved. In his mind, those were just games that he played.

After seeing his family's reactions to his scan, Fallon made the decision to try to change, starting with those who were closest to him. Like many sociopaths, it wasn't that he treated his family terribly, but that he treated them no different, and sometimes worse than he treated a stranger. Most people expect that they will be looked after by those they loved, and given preferential treatment above any stranger you happen to meet, but for a sociopath, there is no emotional attachment and therefore no difference between your family and someone you met yesterday. All that matters is how they can be used to accomplish their own goals and aspirations.

Fallon decided to change how he treated his family, and give them what they expected. To do this was a huge amount of effort for him. Every single time he started to interact with a close friend or family member, he had to stop and think about what a 'normal' person would do, and then force himself to comply. Every action and reaction had to be examined and challenged. What comes so easily to us, the little loving touches and behaviors towards our loved ones throughout the day were completely foreign to Fallon and had to be specifically acted out intellectually.

Interestingly, his family has responded positively. They have been told that he doesn't really mean any of this, that this new kinder self is an intellectual experiment, but they tell him that it doesn't matter, they still like it. Fallon is amazed that merely the action is enough for them, that simply what he was trying was enough. For his part, this experiment is simply another intellectual challenge or pursuit. Dr.

Fallon doesn't believe that anything will come of it, or that he will ever change himself.

When asked why he has ended up the way he has in life, an educated man with a respected job, and married with children, he attributes his success in life to his upbringing. He is quoted as saying he had a 'charmed childhood', and says he wonders how he might have turned out if he'd been abused or mistreated as a child.

So if sociopathy can't be cured, then what are our options? There are treatments available, but if you are involved with the sociopath, it's important for you to make sure your own needs are taken care of first. A sociopath's care provider will often encourage you to stay involved with the sociopath, especially if you are in a romantic relationship with them. In general, sociopaths do better in treatment when they stay involved in their relationship. Despite this, you need to look after yourself, and if staying isn't best for you then do not feel pressured into it.

The first time a sociopath seeks professional help, it is usually because of a co-occurring disorder or court-ordered treatment. Sociopaths are highly unlike to independently seek treatment, or even to respond well to threats or ultimatums to do so from those who love them.

The typical treatment first used is psychotherapy. This treatment focuses on changing behaviors and building skills to deal with situations. Because of a sociopath's inability to understand emotions, psychotherapy for them usually, focuses on helping them better understand how to interact in society. This treatment can involve behavior and cognitive therapy, plus personality restructuring techniques. Psychotherapy remains the recommend primary treatment for sociopathy.

As well as psychological treatments, some may also find medication helpful. Medications do not treat the condition as a whole but instead may be useful in treating other disorders that commonly co-occur with sociopathies, such as anxiety and depression. Medications may also help in reducing violent tendencies and balance moods. Note carefully: (**Reduce and not eliminate)**

Finally, if the sociopath is particularly aggressive or violent, anger management treatment may also be applicable. Again, the effectiveness of this treatment is limited by the sociopath's ability to understand and feel emotions, but a reward and punishment skill building program can be used.

Ultimately, no one can predict how much a sociopath will change under treatment, and at the end, it still may not turn your partner into someone you want to spend the rest of your life with. Treatment can make a person less dangerous, but it cannot make them loving and kind. What you do with that information, and the rest of your life is up to you.

Conclusion

It's an old worn cliché, but when it comes to sociopaths, the most important takeaway from this book is that it wasn't your fault. Sociopaths do not relate to other people, whether you are their friend, their wife or perhaps even their mother. Follow the advice in this book to protect yourself, and what steps to take if you do find yourself involved with a sociopath. Remember, even with treatment, a loving and healthy relationship may well be impossible when dealing with a sociopath, so taking care of yourself first should be your priority.

Once upon a time, sociopathy was hidden in the shadows and was very little understood and studied, it is now becoming more established both by researchers and in popular culture. Movies such as "Bates Motel" and the "Wolf of Wall Street", shows the modern sociopath in a new light. Perhaps even with the newfound knowledge and acceptance of sociopaths, we need to remember that this is not part of a movie, and an encounter with a sociopath in your life can leave you open to true financial and personal ruin or worse. Remember, just because they are not all murderers, doesn't mean that you should overlook their capabilities of becoming one. Be aware, and be safe.

Made in the USA
Las Vegas, NV
22 February 2025